INSIDE THE
OIL
INDUSTRY

by Wil Mara

Content Consultant

Younas Dadmohammadi, PhD

Research Associate
Mewbourne School of Petroleum and
Geological Engineering
University of Oklahoma

Essential Library

An Imprint of Abdo Publishing | abdopublishing.com

abdopublishing.com

Published by Abdo Publishing, a division of ABDO, PO Box 398166, Minneapolis, Minnesota 55439. Copyright © 2017 by Abdo Consulting Group, Inc. International copyrights reserved in all countries. No part of this book may be reproduced in any form without written permission from the publisher. Essential Library™ is a trademark and logo of Abdo Publishing.

Printed in the United States of America, North Mankato, Minnesota
092016
012017

THIS BOOK CONTAINS
RECYCLED MATERIALS

Cover Photo: iStockphoto
Interior Photos: Shutterstock Images, 4, 14, 75; Laura Gangi Pond/Shutterstock Images, 7; Carol and Mike Werner/Science Source, 9; Lonny Garris/Shutterstock Images, 11; Zhu Difeng/Shutterstock Images, 12; George Rinhart/Corbis/Getty Images, 16; Jeremiah Gurney/Beinecke Digital Collections, 18; AP Images, 21, 37, 45, 48, 53, 55, 56; Past Pix/SSPL/Getty Images, 24; Dorling Kindersley/Thinkstock, 27; Time Life Pictures/Mansell/The LIFE Picture Collection/Getty Images, 29; Science Source, 31; Bettmann/Getty Images, 32, 50; Arkivi/Getty Images, 34; Library of Congress, 38–39; Keystone-France/Gamma-Keystone/Getty Images, 41; US Navy, 43; J. R. Eyerman/The LIFE Picture Collection/Getty Images, 46; Bob Daugherty/AP Images, 59; Energy Department/AP Images, 61; Glen Martin/The Denver Post/Getty Images, 62–63; Red Line Editorial, 64, 96–97; US Air Force, 67; Olivier Lantzendorffer/iStockphoto, 68; Tom Hollyman/Science Source, 70; Alberto Loyo/Shutterstock Images, 73; iStockphoto, 77, 86; Anan Kaewkhammul/Shutterstock Images, 78; Newsis/AP Images, 80; Rebecca Blackwell/AP Images, 83; Nils Versemann/Shutterstock Images, 84; Taina Sohlman/iStockphoto, 88–89; Alex Milan Tracy/Sipa USA/AP Images, 91; Signature Message/Shutterstock Images, 93; David Parsons/iStockphoto, 95

Editor: Arnold Ringstad
Series Designer: Craig Hinton

Publisher's Cataloging-in-Publication Data

Names: Mara, Wil, author.
Title: Inside the oil industry / by Wil Mara.
Description: Minneapolis, MN : Abdo Publishing, 2017. | Series: Big business | Includes bibliographical references and index.
Identifiers: LCCN 2016945201 | ISBN 9781680783728 (lib. bdg.) | ISBN 9781680797251 (ebook)
Subjects: LCSH: Petroleum industry and trade --Juvenile literature. | Petroleum products--Juvenile literature.
Classification: DDC 338.2--dc23
LC record available at http://lccn.loc.gov/2016945201

Contents

1 | THE PURSUIT OF INNOVATION

Readers of the *Wall Street Journal* saw an encouraging headline in September 2015: "Oil Companies Tap New Technologies to Lower Production Costs."[1] By the early 2000s, oil had become one of the world's most critical yet most criticized resources. It generated huge amounts of electricity and fueled a majority of the world's cars. But the evidence for its negative impact on the environment—both during extraction and when used—was mounting. Oil was also at the center of international political controversies. Headlines about these negative aspects of oil frequently appeared in newspapers. Now, the *Wall Street Journal* headline was highlighting the ways in which petroleum companies were trying to use technological innovation to improve efficiency and become more environmentally friendly.

The story was about new approaches to oil and gas discovery that industry leaders hoped would make the process less expensive. The efforts were linked to the sinking price of gasoline. By the summer of 2015, prices had dropped to their lowest levels in years. In some parts of the United States, one gallon (3.8 L) of gas could be

For more than a century, oil has powered much of the world's transportation.

purchased for approximately $1.50.[2] Considering the average price just a year before, $3.34 per gallon, it was an astonishing development.[3]

The rise and fall of gasoline prices can have widespread effects on the economy.

Why Did Gasoline Prices Fall in 2015?

The price of gasoline is impossible to predict from day to day, but historical data has shown a clear tendency to experience notably high and low periods. An example of the latter began in 2015. One of the most significant factors for this was an oversupply of oil on the market. Part of the reason for it was overproduction by leading suppliers to meet the perceived needs of expanding middle classes in other countries. Another factor was Iran's reentry into the international oil markets after sanctions enacted by the United States and other nations were lifted following Iran's agreement to abandon its nuclear weapons program in July 2015. With so much excess, prices dropped until the supply-demand ratio returned to balanced levels.

The low prices were good news for consumers but not for the oil companies. With falling prices came falling earnings, and with that came the need to cut jobs. Quicksilver Resources Incorporated, a Texas-based company that drills for raw petroleum and natural gas, was forced to file for bankruptcy in March 2015 and lay off more than 150 members of its workforce. A second Texas outfit, National Oilwell Varco, made plans to cut more than 100 employees and close one of its manufacturing sites.[4] Maersk Drilling, headquartered in Denmark, had to shut down one of its offshore rigs and let all of the rig's workers go. But rather than allow the situation to worsen, companies turned to scientific research to find cheaper ways to bring their product to market.

Regular 429 9/10

Plus 444 9/10

Premium
Diesel 499 9/10

TRYING TO DO BETTER

One innovation from recent years is a process known as refracking. It is similar to the more widely known practice of fracking, or hydraulic fracturing. This method of extracting hydrocarbons involves breaking up large underground rock formations to free as much of the hydrocarbon as possible. Once an initial round of drilling has established early cracks in a formation, fluid is pumped underground at an extremely high pressure to widen the fractures and hold them open. This makes it easier to insert pump lines and draw out the oil that lies beyond.

Refracking is the same concept with one notable twist. Rather than creating new wells, it is used to maximize the production from existing ones. When older and less-capable technologies were unable to extract all the oil from a well the first time, oil companies are able to use refracking to salvage the well. They make tweaks to ensure every possible bit of oil can be retrieved. For example, they use fracking fluids with different viscosities to find the type that works best for a

Hydraulic Fracturing and Earthquakes

There has been much speculation in the media about the seismic dangers of hydraulic fracturing. However, evidence shows the risk of earthquakes from the fracking process itself is low. Many fracking treatments have been carried out in the last 60 years, and yet only a few isolated seismic events have occurred on the surface. However, the United States Geological Survey has determined the disposal of wastewater used in the oil and gas extraction process actually does cause earthquakes. Most of this wastewater is a brine-type fluid that rises from reservoirs during oil and gas production. As it has little use, it is then put back into the ground through injection wells. This increases the pressure underground and can trigger earthquakes.

8

Hydraulic Fracturing

In the hydraulic fracturing process, fluids pumped underground crack rock formations, releasing oil and natural gas. The technique has proven effective and profitable, but it has also proven controversial. It involves moving large amounts of fluid and equipment to the fracking site; this transport can take a toll on the environment. Environmentalists also say fracking is a distraction from the eventual shift to renewable sources of energy.

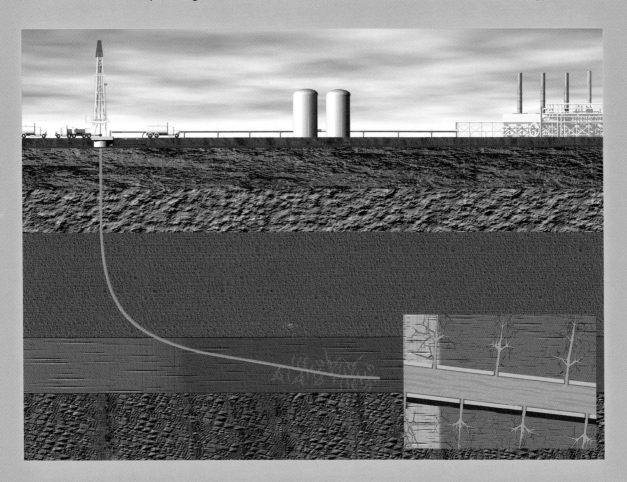

Petroleum and Oil

The terms *petroleum* and *oil* are frequently used synonymously, but there are notable differences in their meaning. Crude petroleum is the dark liquid that occurs in nature as a complex mixture of hydrocarbons. It has a heavy, thick consistency. After being extracted, it is refined into numerous products, including gasoline, propane, butane, asphalt, and a variety of oils. Therefore, the term *oil* is technically a generalization to describe one class of products that can be made from crude. It is also used to describe the material that is sold and shipped in barrels from exporter to importer, as in the phrase, "a barrel of oil." However, this is simply crude petroleum in its raw form. It has not yet been refined as an oil product.

particular reservoir. They seal off existing oil pathways to promote a steadier, smoother flow of the oil that is traveling through new channels.

Fracking and refracking have made vast quantities of previously inaccessible petroleum available.

Refracking can improve efficiency, but it still has many risks and hazards. The production rate of existing reservoirs can potentially be disrupted by the procedure. An adjacent reservoir being used in another well could be ruptured, making the oil in both sites more difficult to reach. The process has also been known to affect drinking water because of the poisonous chemicals often used in the fracking fluid. And there is an ongoing concern that by disturbing the underlying geology of an area, fracking can increase the risk of earthquakes.

However, the potential rewards are significant. Schlumberger Limited, one of the giants in oilfield services, estimated in 2015 that approximately 10,000 horizontal wells drilled during the previous five years alone were prime candidates for refracking.[5] In one case in North Dakota, 80 wells

In many regions, petroleum companies extract oil from underground using machines called pump jacks.

produced roughly 30 percent more oil per month after refracking than before.[6] Unlocking this previously inaccessible potential could be huge news for the petroleum industry.

THE UNDENIABLE POWER OF PETROLEUM

Petroleum is one of the most precious, most widely utilized, and most controversial commodities in the world. It plays a crucial a role in the everyday lives of nearly everyone on Earth. For example, fuel for cars and airplanes is made from petroleum. It's also an essential ingredient in a huge variety of other items, including ink, paint, crayons, pillows, deodorant, aspirin, and vitamins. Petroleum is critical to the production of many plastics too.

Petroleum companies have tremendous power and influence around the world. The key to success in any business is demand, the customers' desire

Natural Gas

When petroleum companies discover untapped reserves underground, they often find extensive reserves of natural gas too. Similar to petroleum, natural gas is a mix of hydrocarbons resulting from the decay of deposited organic matter. In this case, the hydrocarbons form a gas rather than a solid. The bulk of natural gas is a compound known as methane, but there can also be other gases, such as nitrogen and carbon dioxide. Natural gas is often found in shale-rock formations, which hold the gas within their porous structures. To extract the gas, the rock is hydrofractured. This releases the gas to the surface. Natural gas is colorless and odorless. To help people detect it in the event of a potentially dangerous leak, companies add a harmless but foul-smelling chemical to it, giving it an odor similar to rotten eggs.

Many jobs in the petroleum industry, such as working with drilling equipment, involve difficult physical labor.

for whatever that business is offering. The reliance on petroleum products is so enormous that petroleum companies are in a very strong position. They employ millions of workers around the world. In 2015, approximately 192,000 of these workers were in the United States.[7] Petroleum industry facilities often operate around the clock. These corporations earn billions of dollars annually, and their leaders are among the elite in the business world. Petroleum has made some people extremely wealthy. Poor nations that have discovered petroleum under their territory have become rich virtually overnight. At the same time, the political conflicts oil has fueled have driven others into poverty.

The world is beginning to turn away from fossil fuels. These energy sources are derived from ancient living matter buried underground and compressed during the course of millions of years. They come in several forms, including coal, natural gas, and petroleum. As this transition begins, petroleum companies are working to find better and more efficient ways to find, extract, and utilize oil. By applying technological innovation to a large, century-old industry, they seek to keep oil a relevant resource for decades to come.

2 | WHERE IT ALL BEGAN

The Allegheny River runs through Pennsylvania and New York. Feeding into the Allegheny in the northwestern corner of Pennsylvania is a tributary known as Oil Creek. It runs just under 47 miles (76 km).[1] The petroleum industry began in this relatively small stream in August 1859. Oil had been found in seeps along Oil Creek's muddy banks and elsewhere on Earth long before that. Crude, unrefined oil, had been in use in medicines and in flammable weapons for thousands of years. But it was not until August 1859 that people realized oil might have potential beyond this.

The man who put this change into motion was Samuel Kier. In the early 1850s, Kier and his father operated a series of wells for brine, or salty water, in the Pittsburgh, Pennsylvania, area. Their brine was frequently contaminated by oil. Rather than dismiss it as a nuisance, Kier worked with a professor named James Booth to find a way to distill the oil into a useful fuel for lighting. The distilled oil was further treated with chemicals to reduce its unpleasant odor. Kier's idea worked so well others soon began wondering how they could get oil for themselves.

One of those people was a lawyer from New York named George Bissell. He sent an agent to northwestern

In the mid-1850s, the modern oil industry was born in western Pennsylvania.

George Bissell was a major player in the early oil industry.

Pennsylvania in 1854 to study the area. The agent, Yale University chemist Benjamin Sillman Jr., reported oil could be extracted in large amounts. Bissell formed the Pennsylvania Rock Oil Company with friend and fellow lawyer Jonathan Eveleth. He then looked for financial backing from banks and investors. Most investors were skeptical, however. Other businessmen had poured time, money, and energy into the search for oil sources and had little to show for it.

Additionally, there was still uncertainty about possible uses of oil. Sillman made bold predictions, believing oil could be distilled into useful products. To win the confidence of investors, though, the Pennsylvania Rock Oil Company would need to discover a significant source of oil.

EDWIN DRAKE

Finding oil became the job of Edwin Drake. Born in New York to a farming family in 1819, Drake developed a fondness for trains at a young age. He worked in the railway business well into his forties. In the late 1850s, he moved with his wife, Laura, to Titusville, Pennsylvania. Sillman believed oil of a particularly high quality could be found underground there. Drake had suffered health issues and was unable to continue working on the railways, so he was looking for a new challenge. In 1858, the Seneca Oil Company, a competitor of Bissell's firm, hired him to scout several areas in Titusville for ideal places to drill.

Early Uses of Petroleum

There are records of petroleum usage in Mesopotamia in the Middle East dating back thousands of years. The substance was used for everything from medication to road construction. Native Americans also believed it had medicinal value, using it as a treatment for scrapes and cuts. In Europe, it was burned for heat and light, although only sparingly since it was dirty and produced an unpleasant smell. Most cultures seemed to regard it as little more than a curiosity. But in the mid-1800s, the increased demand for light, lubrication, and fuel led to more research into oil's possibilities. Within decades, it would become one of the world's most widely used resources.

Drake eventually focused on a small island within Oil Creek, in part because local Native Americans told stories of black medicine in the ground.

Drake, right, stands before his oil well.

He began purchasing drilling equipment and hiring laborers. Because of the extreme limits of drilling technology at the time, the well progressed at the agonizing pace of a few feet per day. By August 1859, Drake's borehole was approximately 65 feet (20 m) deep, and still there was no oil.[2] Local residents who were at first curious about the venture now dismissed it. Even Drake's supporters at the Seneca Company had abandoned the project, leaving him with virtually no money to carry on. Maintaining his belief in the well, Drake turned to friends for financial aid. One of the few who stayed with him was blacksmith William Smith.

The Fate of Edwin Drake

Despite Edwin Drake's mark on history, much of the remainder of his life was filled with bad breaks and difficult circumstances. He failed to invest in the oil industry, missing out on a chance to get rich. In fact, he left the Seneca Oil Company in 1860 with a payment of just $1,000.[4] By 1865, he was broke and in failing health. Drake's life came to an end in November 1880 following years of health issues and financial woes.

On August 27, with the well at 69 feet (21 m), work ended for the day.[3] A dejected Drake headed home. No activity was scheduled for the following day, a Sunday, but Smith returned to the site anyway to inspect the equipment. When he arrived he saw oil running out the top of the pipe. Returning to the site the next day, Drake found Smith and the other workers struggling to contain as much oil as possible in barrels, buckets, jars, and any other containers they could find.

Following this historic oil strike, the petroleum industry spread through Pennsylvania like wildfire. It was not long before other states began getting into the game, frantically building wells and filling barrels to keep up with demand for the new lighting fuel. By the 1870s, West Virginia, Ohio, and California were producing thousands of barrels per year. Within ten more years, New York, Kentucky, and Tennessee joined the club of major oil-producing states.

The newborn petroleum industry was disorganized and chaotic. In the race to stake claims and get the product out of the ground, there had been few efforts to increase efficiency or centralization. That would soon change with the arrival of John D. Rockefeller, who established the Standard Oil Company in 1870 in Ohio.

Through Standard, Rockefeller bought out competing companies, drastically cut operating costs, sold at prices so low that remaining competitors were driven into bankruptcy, and even

A Booming Industry

Wells sprang up as fast as they could be built following Drake's breakthrough. The output from Pennsylvania alone rose from approximately 4,500 barrels in 1859 to 220,000 in 1860. This figure jumped to more than 2,100,000 in 1861.[5] By 1869, ten years after the Drake strike, Pennsylvania was producing more than four million barrels per year.[6] Americans were not the only ones taking note of this remarkable development. In Europe, where industrialized mechanization was also progressing at a healthy pace, the need for petroleum products was growing right along with it. As a result, the United States began sending more petroleum overseas than it was using at home. Petroleum soon became one of the United States' leading exports.

developed his own infrastructure of oil pipelines to reduce his dependency on railways. Many people resented Rockefeller's cutthroat tactics. They moved to stop him either through legal methods, such as lawsuits or boycotts, or illegal ones, such as destruction of property. However, the company had become so big the only entity large and powerful enough to take action against it would be the US government.

John D. Rockefeller

John D. Rockefeller was born to humble beginnings on July 8, 1839, in Richmond, New York. His mother, Eliza, was devoutly religious. His father, Bill, was a professional con artist who spent long stretches on the road and away from his family. Young John was more like his mother, religious and serious, and he had a natural gift for mathematics. His first job, at the age of 16, was as a bookkeeper. He soon took an interest in the rapidly evolving petroleum industry. By 1869, he and some partners had built oil refineries in Cleveland, Ohio. The following year, Rockefeller formed the Standard Oil Company. He would soon become the central figure in the industry.

3 | INCREASING DEMAND

More than any other vehicle, automobiles have become emblematic of the use of oil as fuel. But the earliest automobiles used other sources of power, such as steam or electricity. They entered widespread use by the late 1800s. For a time, electric cars were the preferred mode of personal transport, as they ran more smoothly and reliably than the earlier steam-powered cars, which required frequent attention. Nevertheless, the steam car and the electric car would soon begin losing popularity to a new invention: cars with internal combustion engines.

Internal combustion engines burn fuel to create a continuous series of tiny explosions that drive pistons. The movement of the pistons is translated into movement in the wheels, pushing the car forward. For years, various fuels were tried in this type of engine with little success. Then German engineer and inventor Karl Benz turned to an engine that ran on gasoline, a by-product of petroleum distillation. Benz thought it would be ideal for use with the automobile, so he built a prototype vehicle in 1885. He received a patent for it the next year and began producing his cars for sale in 1888 following a 50-mile (80 km) demonstration drive that showcased the vehicle's safety.[1]

Early steam-powered automobiles were never as widespread as their gasoline-powered successors.

Early Steam-Powered Automobiles

Frenchman Nicolas-Joseph Cugnot built the first steam-powered car in 1769. Cugnot was an inventor and military engineer. His design had three wheels and a giant boiler hanging from the front. Cugnot built another a year later, this one meant to carry military supplies, and a third the year after that. None of the designs turned out to be practical, so the military did not use them. Another French inventor, Amédée Bollée, pursued the notion of a steam-powered passenger vehicle again in 1873. Bollée designed one that had a steering wheel and an iron-riveted body. It could carry a dozen people.

In 1895, seven years after Benz began manufacturing, the first US car company was founded. Brothers Charles and Frank Duryea established the Duryea Motor Wagon Company. The company produced only 13 vehicles in its first three years, but the brothers had spurred a trend.[2] Other companies began springing up to take advantage of the rising demand for automobiles. This was accompanied by a matching increase in demand for the gasoline to fuel these cars.

THE GASOLINE FACTOR

Gasoline is a by-product of petroleum made through a process known as fractional distillation. Fractional distillation is the separation of any type of mixture into its basic components. In the case of crude oil, the original substance separates into different parts through extreme heating and pressurization. Many things used in daily life are produced from crude oil, including gases such as methane, propane, and butane, solids such as grease and Vaseline, heavy fluids such as lubricating oil, and light fluids such as kerosene and gasoline. In many cases, these separated components are treated with chemical additives to improve their quality. Gasoline, for example, has additives to increase the efficiency of its combustion and reduce engine corrosion.

The battle for dominance between steam, electric, and gasoline vehicles raged until the 1910s, when the gas-powered cars pulled ahead and internal combustion engines continued to improve

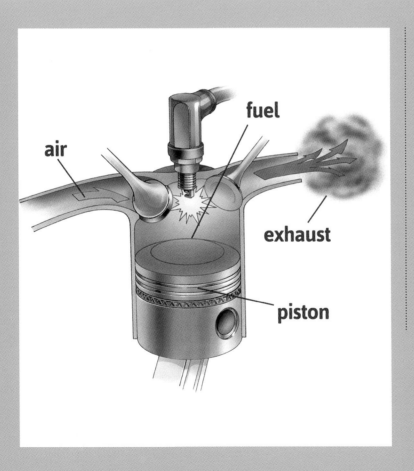

air

fuel

exhaust

piston

Internal Combustion Engines

Internal combustion engines take in air, compress it in a cylinder, add fuel, and ignite the mixture to push a piston downward. The movement of the piston is turned into rotational motion that is transferred to the wheels. As the piston pushes back upward, it forces the leftover gases, or exhaust, out of the engine. The entire process repeats several times per second for each of the engine's cylinders.

Beyond the Engine

As more experimentation and innovation was devoted to cars with internal combustion engines in the early 1900s, other technological advances found their way into the vehicles. Early cars had tillers, single bars that drivers could rotate to turn the wheels. Gradually, steering wheels replaced them, because the tillers were unsafe at high speeds. Early models used a crankshaft to start the engine, a dangerous method that produced sparks. This was replaced by safer and easier-to-use electric ignition systems. Drum brakes became a reliable way of bringing a car to a halt. Shock-absorption springs made for a much more comfortable ride on bumpy roads, as paving had not yet become widespread.

in efficiency. As the automobile industry developed in the early 1900s, Standard Oil continued to grow in power and influence until it was the undisputed leader in the petroleum market. It ran its refineries around the clock, bought or forced out most competitors, and emphasized efficiency. It had customers around the world, including in China, Japan, and parts of the Middle East.

Rockefeller had a clear stranglehold on the oil industry at this point, a condition known as a monopoly. Many began to criticize Rockefeller and his company. One of those people was journalist Ida Tarbell. Tarbell was born in northwestern Pennsylvania in 1857. Three years later, her family moved to Titusville. There, her father started working in the rapidly growing oil business, first as a builder and then as a refiner. In the 1870s, however, her father's company went under due in part to the underhanded tactics of Rockefeller and Standard Oil. Rockefeller made a deal with the Pennsylvania Railroad to exclusively transport his own output as well as that of other large refiners.

John D. Rockefeller built history's first oil empire.

Smaller refiners, such as the one run by Tarbell's father, could not get in on the deal, forcing the majority of them out of business.

Tarbell never forgot or forgave Rockefeller. Although she began her professional life as a teacher, she discovered a talent for writing and began putting together articles for magazines.

One of the publications she wrote for was *McClure's* magazine. Issues came out once a month, were fully illustrated, and often included in-depth pieces that are today considered pioneering works in the field of investigative journalism. It was through this powerful media platform that Tarbell realized she had an opportunity to settle the score with John D. Rockefeller.

STANDARD GOES DOWN

Tarbell began looking into Rockefeller's business affairs in 1900. For the next two years, she sifted through thousands of pages of documents while interviewing anyone and everyone who could provide useful information, including those who had worked for Rockefeller and those who harbored resentment against him. The result of her research was a series of articles that ran in *McClure's* from 1902 to 1904. The pieces spanned 19 separate issues and shed light on Rockefeller's ruthless practices.[3] Rockefeller grew to fiercely resent the woman, calling her "Miss Tar Barrel" to his friends.[4] But the public's reaction to the articles was strong and immediate, quickly turning Rockefeller into one of the most disliked figures in the United States. The public encouraged the US government to take action.

In 1890, the US Congress passed the Sherman Antitrust Act. It got its name from John Sherman, the Ohio senator who drafted the bulk of the text. The act attempted to eliminate business activities the government believed to be anticompetitive. Not long after taking office, President Theodore Roosevelt ordered his government to strongly enforce the Sherman Antitrust Act, and one of the companies he wanted to target was Standard Oil. The case against Rockefeller quickly

Standard Oil was headquartered in New York City.

became a contentious affair, with Rockefeller acting impatient and cranky every time he had to appear in court. He argued he had transformed a chaotic industry into one of order and efficiency. But these attempts to cast himself in a noble light fell on deaf ears.

The US Supreme Court handed down the final judgment on May 15, 1911. The court found Standard Oil in violation of the Sherman Antitrust Act and ordered it to be broken into 34 separate companies.[5] The Rockefeller-dominated era in the history of the oil industry had come to a close.

The Sherman Antitrust Act

The word *antitrust* in the name of the Sherman Antitrust Act refers specifically to corporate trusts, which are groups of large businesses that join together to control a specific market, thus forcing out smaller and weaker competitors. Before the 1900s, the act was used relatively little. President William McKinley, for example, who held office from 1897 until 1901, was considered a friend of big business and was hesitant to exercise the act's power. After McKinley's assassination on September 14, 1901, his vice president, Theodore Roosevelt, became president. Roosevelt believed strongly in breaking up companies that were rigging the system against smaller rivals.

4 | OIL AND WARFARE

The rise of the automobile showed oil was becoming an increasingly important commodity in the early 1900s. But the two world wars fought in this era made it clear that ownership and control of oil was directly linked to a nation's power and wealth.

For hundreds of years, horses were the fastest means of travel for soldiers. Troops used cannons, firearms, and bladed weapons. World War I (1914–1918) ushered in a new age of warfare that depended tremendously on a steady supply of oil and its by-products. Many of the war's leaders realized oil and its uses could provide significant advantages. At the onset of World War I, Winston Churchill helped oversee the United Kingdom's Royal Navy. He was faced with the decision of whether to convert some British ships from using coal to using fuel oil. The Royal Navy had already made this conversion on submarines and destroyers. And even in coal-powered ships, oil was being added to the coal to improve combustibility. Churchill had to decide if the nation would take it one step further, committing larger vessels such as battleships to oil.

One of the most daunting barriers Churchill faced was the fact that while the United Kingdom already had

Enormous battleships, including the United Kingdom's HMS Queen Elizabeth, were among the many weapons of war that required vast oil resources to operate.

War Drives Innovation

Innovations in the field of refining developed before World War I were an important factor in the evolution of the industry. For example, two significant processes created in 1913 helped to significantly boost gasoline supplies. German chemist Friedrich Karl Rudolf Bergius discovered a way of creating a viable synthetic fuel by processing coal at high pressures and temperatures. The end product was not utilized by Germany during World War I, but it would play a role in World War II. The other major 1913 development involved two chemists working for Standard Oil, William Burton and Robert Humphreys. They developed a method of refinement known as thermal cracking, which breaks down heavy petroleum molecules into lighter ones through heat and pressure during the distillation process. The new process allowed for large increases in gasoline production.

a reliable coal-supplying infrastructure, it had little infrastructure for oil. The ships that used coal had mechanisms in place to accommodate it and crewmen trained to handle it. Coal also had the benefit of not exploding when taking enemy fire. But Churchill eventually focused on coal's many problems rather than its advantages. Moving coal from supply trucks onto vessels took a tremendous amount of time and effort, which in turn tired out sailors whose energy was needed elsewhere. He said, "The ordeal of coaling [a] ship exhausted the whole ship's company. In wartime it robbed them of their brief period of rest; it subjected everyone to extreme discomfort."[1] Further, a ship in need of more coal could not simply refuel at sea. It had to travel to the nearest friendly port with an ample supply. Also, handling and burning coal was a particularly filthy affair, endangering the health of those who had to deal with it.

Churchill's plan to shift from coal to oil was controversial at the time, but in hindsight it was a key turning point in naval history.

A SOLUTION TO THE PROBLEM

The tank was among the newly developed weapons powered by oil during World War I.

Fuel oil eliminated these problems and offered further benefits. Ships running on it could travel greater distances at faster speeds. The boilers for burning oil did not have to be as large as those fired by coal. Oil produced less smoke, making ships less visible to the enemy. Oil could be channeled through pipes and tubes, requiring fewer men to manage it. And when refueling was required, tanker ships could be sent to critical areas and fuel multiple vessels in a single outing.

Around the same time the United Kingdom was transitioning its naval boats to oil, its ally the United States was doing likewise. Its enemy Germany, on the other hand, did not fully realize oil's potential in ships until after the war ended. This gave the United Kingdom and the United States a distinct advantage. The use of oil in

the Royal Navy was not the make-or-break factor in the war, but it certainly helped. Oil played important roles throughout the war's many battlefields. It kept planes in the air, ships moving through the sea, and cars and trucks on the road. It also fueled new armored fighting machines known as tanks.

As the demand for oil during the war increased, production worldwide increased as well. In Iran alone, production increased by ten times between 1912 and 1914. The United States also entered the picture, eventually supplying up to 80 percent of the oil needs of the United Kingdom and its allies.[2] The United States' role in supplying oil reached a point where the nation was sending a quarter of its output overseas. It needed even more oil after formally entering the war in April 1917. Shortages were all but inevitable. The government had to make arrangements with domestic companies, including those that were once part of Standard Oil. Many Americans reduced their usage of oil products as a way of contributing to the war effort.

At the same time the Allies sought to boost their own oil production, they worked to cut off

A Question of Supply

Using oil in navy vessels had clear benefits, but Churchill faced obstacles in implementing the plan. One of the most significant was finding a steady supply of oil. A British delegation was sent to the Persian Gulf and eventually chose the Anglo-Persian Oil Company (APOC) as its supplier. The England-based company had been established after the 1908 discovery of a major oilfield in southern Iran. Through Churchill's influence, the British government made a deal with APOC to ensure a reliable flow during the war effort under financial terms favorable to the British.

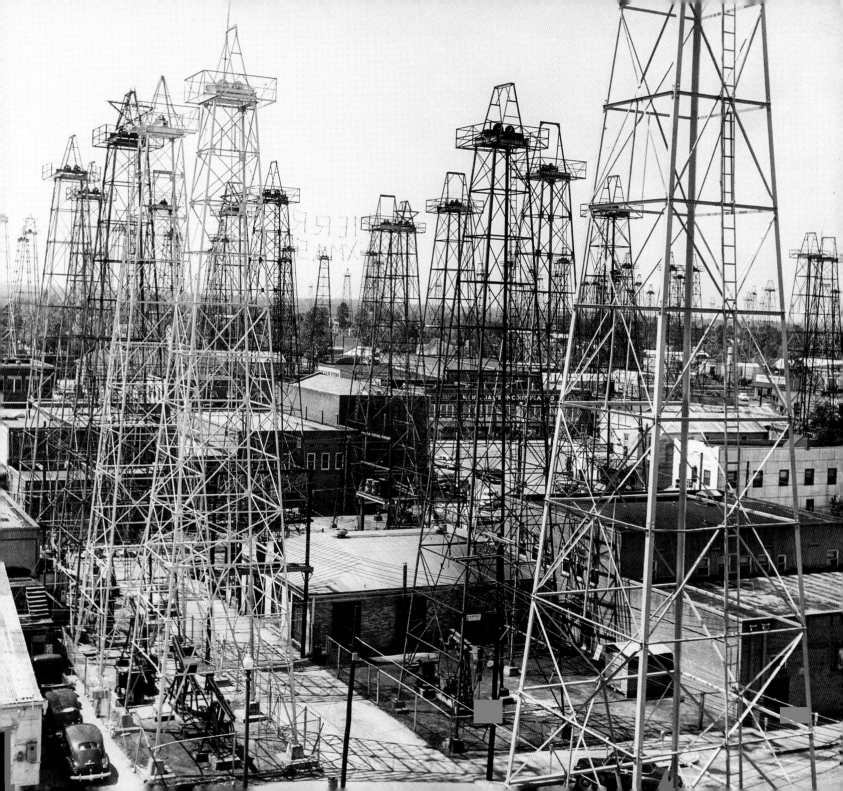

their enemy's supply. When Germany's major supplier was the nation of Romania, the British attacked and destroyed approximately 70 refineries there.[3] By the fall of 1918, with its oil supplies nearing exhaustion, Germany surrendered and the war came to an end. French senator Henry Bérenger said at the time, "Oil, the blood of the Earth, was the blood of victory. . . . Germany had boasted too much of its superiority in iron and coal, but it had not taken sufficient account of our superiority in oil. . . . As oil had been the blood of war, so it would be the blood of the peace."[4]

New technologies, including aircraft carriers and the planes they carried, increased the military demand for oil even higher than it had been during World War I.

ONE WAR LEADS TO ANOTHER

Oil production dropped significantly in the aftermath of the war as military demand decreased. However, petroleum continued to play an important role in the world economy. Automobiles became more widespread, war-torn nations rebuilt their devastated infrastructures, and engineers found more uses for the ever-improving internal combustion engine.

When World War II (1939–1945) broke out, triggered by the German invasion of Poland, oil again played a critical role. The United Kingdom and France quickly declared war on Germany. This time there would be no debates about coal versus oil—everything was running on oil, and once more the governments turned to their domestic petroleum companies for help. The United States entered the war in December 1941 after Japan, Germany's ally, attacked the US naval base at Pearl Harbor, Hawaii. President Franklin D. Roosevelt soon formed the Petroleum Administration for War, and the leader of that administration, Harold Ickes, handpicked more than 70 leaders in the

oil industry to help assure the oil demands of the United States and its allies would be satisfied.[5] New pipelines were laid from Texas to the East Coast to assure a steady and uninterrupted flow.

In the later years of World War II, bombers by the hundreds slammed German oil infrastructure throughout Europe.

American Targeting of German Oil

During World War II, the United States and its allies undertook numerous strategic bombings on critical sites in Germany. This included aircraft factories, ammunition storage depots, and military bases. It also included significant targets related to German oil supplies. Fuel for Germany's air forces came from a dozen refineries scattered around the country. Attacks on these plants began in August 1943, and by July of the following year, each one had been heavily damaged. This was a massive blow to the German war effort. The shortage played an important role in Germany's loss.

This time around, oil helped in more ways than fueling tanks, trucks, ships, and planes. A petroleum by-product called toluene was needed in mass quantities as a critical component in the manufacturing of explosives. An inexpensive form of synthetic rubber made from oil was used after Japanese forces seized 90 percent of the world's natural rubber supply in what is now Indonesia.[6]

As in World War I, attacking the enemy's oil infrastructure was one of the keys to victory. In Europe, the United States and the United Kingdom launched hundreds of bombing raids against German refineries. Germany surrendered in May of 1945, and Japan surrendered in September. As the world neared the century's midpoint, oil had become one of the most important commodities on the planet.

5 | THE RISE OF THE EAST

In the years immediately following World War II, the United States sat comfortably atop the petroleum industry. It was the world's largest oil supplier and user. The United Kingdom and the Netherlands were among the other major players in the industry. However, other countries soon began to discover and take advantage of their own oil reserves. Resentment toward the longtime industry leaders was growing.

BREAKING POINT

Iran was one of the first countries to make a move to counter the dominant oil nations. The British, after setting up an oil company there in 1908, had taken most of the profits from Iran's vast oil reserves. As the years passed and it became obvious their nation possessed enormous oil resources, the Iranians tried to get the British to give them a greater percentage of the rewards. British negotiators were reluctant to concede much. Over time an ugly tension between the two sides arose. The situation was further inflamed in December 1950 when Iran's leadership learned the United States, in a similar deal with Saudi Arabia, had agreed to split oil profits down the middle. A strong feeling of national pride had been on the rise in Iran since the end of World War II. Many of its people began

By the 1950s, cities across the United States were building superhighways to carry huge volumes of cars. As cars became central to US life, oil demand increased.

Frustrated Iranian demonstrators occupied an Anglo-Iranian Oil Company building in 1951.

looking upon British oil activities in their country as greed-driven exploitation. By 1951, there was a strong sentiment in Iran to remove the United Kingdom from the picture by giving the government ownership of the domestic oil industry. In March of 1951, the Iranian parliament voted to do just that.

The United Kingdom's reaction was immediate and dramatic. It pulled its workforce out of the country, bringing production to a near standstill. It froze all Iranian assets within its banking system. And it halted the export of all goods to Iran. Realizing the decay of this relationship could have serious global implications, the United States urged the United Kingdom to be more generous in its arrangement with the Iranians. Iran's government, pressured by heightened feelings of nationalistic pride, refused all offers. The unfortunate consequence of this decision was a struggling Iranian economy dependent on oil revenues.

As the 1950s progressed and Iran's economic conditions continued to worsen, bitterness toward the top seven oil companies, nicknamed the Seven Sisters, grew to a fever pitch. Iran had no intention of returning to the conditions of the former arrangement. In the end, the United Kingdom's company, British Petroleum, agreed to join a larger group of companies that included US, French, and Dutch partners. Together they would strike a deal with the newly formed National Iranian Oil Company, which involved an evenly split share of all profits. Even so, under the terms of the new deal, the Iranians were not allowed to examine the consortium's accounting records. The foreign group

The Seven Sisters

The seven companies that made up the Seven Sisters were the Anglo Persian Oil Company, Gulf Oil, Royal Dutch Shell, Standard Oil of California, Standard Oil of New Jersey, Standard Oil of New York, and Texaco. The term *Seven Sisters* was introduced by Italian businessman Enrico Mattei, who was at one time the head of the government agency that oversaw Italy's petroleum affairs. Mattei started a chemical business as a young man, and it made him very wealthy. He later played a key role in negotiations on oil contracts with other countries, including Egypt, Iran, France, and Spain.

By the 1950s, Iran had vast infrastructure in place for collecting and processing oil.

could report whatever numbers it pleased. This created another layer of tension between the Iranians and the Seven Sisters.

Iran had already been in conversation with a few of the smaller players in the global oil community, including Venezuela, Iraq, and Saudi Arabia, for several years. They shared a concern that continued dominance by the Seven Sisters could lead to greater problems. The breaking point likely came in February 1959, when the Seven Sisters decided to make a 10 percent reduction in the price of oil from Venezuela and several Middle Eastern producers without consulting any of them beforehand.[1] The hostility resulting from this move led to a September 1960 meeting in Baghdad, Iraq, of top industry figures from Iran, Iraq, Kuwait, Saudi Arabia, and Venezuela. Out of this meeting came a new organization called the Organization of the Petroleum Exporting Countries (OPEC).

THE FIRST MAJOR MOVE

In the late spring and early summer of 1967, OPEC made a move to test its power. On June 5, a war broke out between Israel and three neighboring countries, Egypt, Jordan, and Syria. Tensions had

In OPEC's Own Words

OPEC describes its official mandate as:

The mission of the Organization of the Petroleum Exporting Countries (OPEC) is to coordinate and unify the petroleum policies of its Member Countries and ensure the stabilization of oil markets in order to secure an efficient, economic and regular supply of petroleum to consumers, a steady income to producers, and a fair return on capital for those investing in the petroleum industry.[2]

been running high since the arrival of Jewish settlers following World War II. The 1967 conflict was sparked by Israeli reaction to a buildup of Egyptian forces along their shared border, specifically in an area known as the Sinai Peninsula. Working with better-trained soldiers and a more carefully considered strategy, Israel forged an overwhelming victory despite being outnumbered more than two to one. Israel not only forced its enemies to retreat, but it inflicted more than 20,000 fatalities while limiting its own to less than 1,000.[3] The conflict became known as the Six-Day War.

OPEC's involvement in the conflict was direct and dramatic. On the second day of fighting, the organization announced it would place an embargo on oil shipments to any nation that was seen as aiding the Israelis. This bold move effectively established OPEC not only as an industrial

OPEC's First Years

In the years immediately following OPEC's formation, the organization created a leadership position with the title of secretary general. While this individual would act as a manager and overseer for the organization, he or she would not possess absolute controlling authority. Instead, the secretary general would act as the face of the organization, dealing with other organizations and countries on OPEC's behalf while taking direction from the true guiding body, the Board of Governors. The secretary general would also try to moderate disputes between member nations.

OPEC set up its headquarters in Geneva, Switzerland. It moved to the Austrian capital of Vienna in September 1965, where it remained in 2016. OPEC allowed other nations to join the group. The Seven Sisters' home countries were not considered, but the doors were opened to Qatar in 1961, Libya and Indonesia in 1962, the United Arab Emirates in 1967, and Algeria in 1969. The organization felt the larger it became, the more leverage it would have against the powerful Seven Sisters.

Israeli tank crews and other troops defeated forces from three Arab nations, resulting in the Israeli takeover of the Sinai Peninsula.

consortium, but a political one. In this instance, the embargo was aimed specifically at the United States and the United Kingdom.

OPEC's Early Leaders

OPEC's first secretary general was an Iranian, Fuad Rouhani, who held the office from January 1961 to April 1964. Educated as a lawyer, Rouhani's first positions in the oil industry were during the days of British oversight, and he eventually played a role in guiding his government toward nationalization. Known for a calm, moderate nature, he helped shape the early profile of OPEC, including the establishment of its first headquarters in Switzerland. Following Rouhani's leadership, OPEC members chose an Iraqi named Abd al-Rahman al-Bazzaz to succeed him in 1964. Al-Bazzaz was more fiery in nature than Rouhani. Also trained as a lawyer, al-Bazzaz had strong legal, political, and religious views, and spent much of his adult life trying to manifest them in public policy. He was a firm believer in creating unity among Arab nations and had a fierce opposition to influence from the West. He was the dean of Baghdad Law College as well as Iraq's prime minister before replacing Rouhani at OPEC.

This first attempt at flexing the organization's muscle met with minimal success and in some ways backfired. The United States conferred with industrial leaders in friendly nations and formed a response committee to find solutions to the problem. By increasing imports from other nations, the United States was able to get around the embargo. Another factor was the uncertainty among OPEC nations concerning how much oil to withhold. Syria was the only one to cease its exports entirely. A final difficulty was that the countries that reduced their exports to the United States and the United Kingdom suffered economically. These two nations were among the world's largest oil customers.

All embargo tactics came to an end following a meeting among Arab leaders in the Sudanese capital of Khartoum from August 29 to September 1, 1967. Normal business relationships resumed upon the signing of the Khartoum Resolution, although the document had clear

Based in Vienna, Austria, OPEC began flexing its economic muscles in the late 1960s.

language confirming the ongoing hostility of the Arab states toward Israel. Though this first attempt by OPEC did not produce the desired results, it did provide valuable lessons the organization would use to its benefit in the years ahead.

6 | OIL SHORTAGES

With the relationship between the West and the Arab states particularly tense, the 1970s rapidly developed into a historic era of multiple energy crises. The intertwined issues of oil supply and demand sat squarely at the heart of these disputes. At the same time, the nature of the petroleum industry changed, as did the power structure of the world's leading nations. These developments set the tone for oil's role in the world for years to come.

At the start of the 1970s, the United States faced difficult circumstances. First, its oil output began a slow downward trajectory, resulting in the country becoming more dependent upon oil supplies from foreign nations. Increasing demand for oil worsened the problem. There were more cars on the road than ever before, and fuel efficiency was not yet a focus for auto manufacturers. Oil also had hundreds of other uses, for everything from building materials and road construction to the wide selection of retail products made with oil by-products. These factors, combined with the ever-expanding influence of OPEC and continuing tensions in the Middle East, made for a tense situation.

Oil crises in the 1970s had a sharp impact on daily life in the United States.

OPEC's first attempt at an embargo in 1967 met with limited success, but its second would have a very different effect. The spark for it was essentially the same—a military struggle between Israel and its neighbors. It began on October 6, 1973, when forces from Egypt and Syria attacked Israeli forces in two critical areas—the Sinai Peninsula and the Golan Heights. Israel had occupied and claimed both areas following the Six-Day War in 1967. The Arab forces launched their attack on the Jewish holy day of Yom Kippur, which led to the naming of the conflict as the Yom Kippur War. Battles raged for weeks with heavy losses on both sides. The United States decided to assist Israel.

US secretary of state Henry Kissinger spoke to the news media about the US intention not to give in to the OPEC oil embargo.

A SECOND EMBARGO

OPEC immediately placed an embargo on oil exports to the United States and the Netherlands, Israel's closest European ally. OPEC's hope was to force the United States to drop its support for

Life in America during the 1973 Crisis

The oil crisis of 1973 caused significant disruptions in daily life for many in the United States. For example, there were bans on gas-consuming luxury activities such as boating and private airplane flights. Some places forbade unnecessary driving on Saturdays or Sundays. Gas stations began rationing on certain days of the week, or on alternating days based on the last digit of a vehicle's license-plate number. The government urged people to cut back on power use in general, encouraging practices such as turning off lights and setting thermostats a little lower than usual. There was a drop in the nationwide speed limit to 55 miles per hour (89 kmh).[1] The gas crunch also led to fights at gas stations and the theft of gasoline. Many car manufacturers began equipping new vehicles with locks on the gas tanks.

Operation Nickel Grass

President Richard Nixon approved assistance for Israel during the Yom Kippur War in a plan known as Operation Nickel Grass. It came as the United States was ending its involvement in the Vietnam War (1955–1975). The United States sent tanks and ammunition to the Israeli military, partially in response to shipments of supplies the Egyptian and Syrian forces received from the Soviet Union. At first, Israel employed commercial aircraft from its national airline to bring equipment from the United States. It soon became obvious this would not be enough. In response to Israeli prime minister Golda Meir's requests for more assistance, Nixon authorized US aircraft to airlift in supplies. With many nations unwilling to get involved in the conflict, the US cargo planes had to chart courses that avoided those nations' airspace.

Israel. However, doing so would leave Israel in a position of such military vulnerability that defeat would be almost guaranteed. US president Richard Nixon had no intention of seeing this happen. An attempt by OPEC to negotiate an increase in the price of its oil worsened the situation. These negotiations began two days after the start of the Yom Kippur War and ended with Western nations refusing to agree. Nevertheless, on October 16, with the war still raging, six Arab countries announced they would raise their prices while also reducing production levels. OPEC was attempting to use oil as a weapon.

The Yom Kippur War reached its conclusion on October 26, 1973, with a negotiated cease-fire. Bitterness on both sides continued. The following month, Arab oil producers announced they would be cutting production a further 25 percent.[2] Less than a week later, President Nixon signed the Emergency Petroleum Allocation Act, which empowered the government to control the price

The Strategic Petroleum Reserve is held at multiple sites in the United States, including at a facility in Bryan Mound, Texas.

and distribution of petroleum products within the United States. Still, the impact of the embargo on the US economy was significant. Since oil was integrated into nearly every sector, there was a dramatic shift in manufacturing, construction, retail sales, services, and many other parts of the economy. Gasoline shortages were rampant throughout the country as prices rose and supplies dwindled.

The government began viewing the problem with a forward-thinking perspective, and some of the steps it took have continued to shape the petroleum industry today. Perhaps the most significant was the establishment of the Strategic Petroleum Reserve (SPR). This is a large reserve of domestic petroleum for use during national emergencies. The SPR was part of a broader effort by the US government to increase its domestic energy supplies and reduce its dependence on foreign sources. The overall effort was outlined in the Energy Policy and Conservation Act. The act was presented to Congress in February of 1975 and signed into law by President Gerald R. Ford the following December. Other elements of the bill included strategies for increased energy efficiency, reduced demand and usage, and expanded presidential powers to react to crises in the future. All of these measures played a significant role in shaping US energy policy in the years ahead.

The Ford Tempo was among the first popular cars specifically designed for fuel efficiency.

THEN TO NOW

Spurred by ongoing instability among its Middle Eastern oil suppliers, the United States continued searching for alternative approaches to its energy demands. In the early 1980s, car

US Oil Consumption by Sector, 1949–2015

Since 1949, the amount of petroleum used for transportation in the United States has largely steadily increased. The share of petroleum for other uses has remained stable or even fallen.

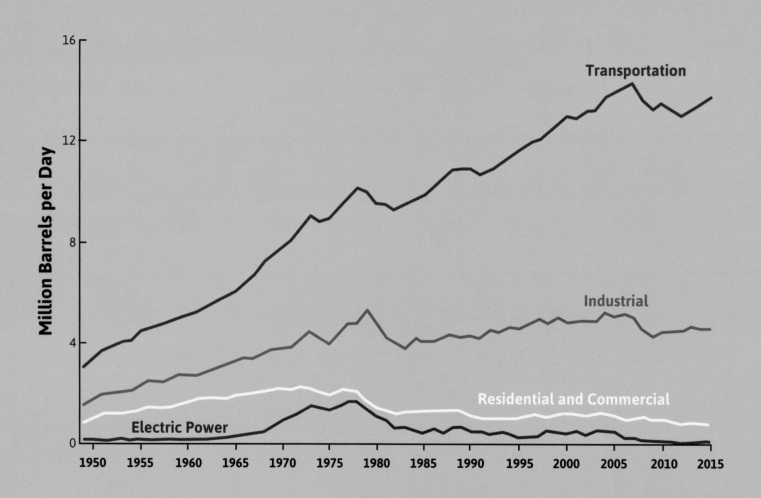

manufacturers began experimenting with vehicles that were smaller and more fuel-efficient than most models of the time. A notable example of this was the Ford Tempo, which the Ford Motor Company introduced in 1984. It was considered a compact car, smaller than typical midsize vehicles. The Tempo featured a four-cylinder engine and an aerodynamic design to improve fuel efficiency.

The government, led by President Jimmy Carter, also supported domestic oil companies in their search for new oil fields at home, including many offshore sites and numerous locations in Alaska. It also supported the development of alternative energy sources, those that do not use fossil fuels. These include nuclear, solar, wind, hydroelectric, geothermal, biomass, and others.

OPEC lost some of its power in the 1980s. With demand shrinking because of actions in the United States and elsewhere, its position declined. The Soviet Union also stepped up its own production

Another Crisis

The energy crises of the 1970s hit another peak in 1979 as a result of the Iranian Revolution. Many Iranians, including students and extremist Islamic organizations, rejected the nation's leader, Mohammed Reza Shah Pahlavi. Pahlavi had been in power since 1941, and he was favorable toward the West in a way many of his people found unacceptable. Aggressive opposition toward his administration began in earnest with public demonstrations in late 1977 and climaxed with his exile in January 1979. The new administration, led by revolutionary leader Ayatollah Ruhollah Khomeini, marked the beginning of an era of strong Islamic influence and anti-Western sentiment. The revolution, as well as the Iran–Iraq War (1980–1988), caused significant interruptions in oil supply to world markets.

OPEC's Cousin

The 1968 creation of a second Arab-based petroleum coalition, the Organization of Arab Petroleum Exporting Countries (OAPEC), further increased tensions between East and West. The principal founders of this new entity were Kuwait, Libya, and Saudi Arabia. OPEC members that were not from the region, such as Venezuela, were not invited to join. By 2016, the organization had 11 member nations.[5]

and soon became the top supplier in the world. By the mid-1980s, there was an excess of oil, which brought down prices. A spike in oil prices occurred in 1990, driven by market panic in the wake of Iraqi dictator Saddam Hussein's invasion of Kuwait. But prices settled back down relatively rapidly, reaching historic lows at the dawn of the new millennium. By the early 2000s, prices were once again on the rise, driven upward by ongoing tensions in the Middle East, increasing demand from China, and speculation in world financial markets that a collapse was on the horizon. Oil prices edged upward to $135 per barrel.[3] In the United States, the highest prices for gasoline reached just under $8.00 per gallon in some areas of Alaska in July 2008.[4] At those levels, many economic sectors became sluggish as the cost of doing business skyrocketed, leading to millions of job layoffs. Per-barrel prices would not drop significantly until the mid-2010s. At this time, another supply glut came about in part from the return of Iranian oil to the market after international sanctions against the country were lifted in July 2015.

As US troops and warplanes beat back Saddam Hussein's 1990 invasion of Kuwait, retreating Iraqi forces set fire to Kuwait's oil wells.

7 | HOW IT ALL WORKS TODAY

The contemporary petroleum industry is a vast and complex system with interconnected corporations, millions of workers, and a greater impact on people's daily lives than ever before. Oil plays critical roles in the world's economy and politics. It is likely the most important natural resource of the last century.

The petroleum industry is commonly viewed in three distinct sectors—upstream, midstream, and downstream. The lines between them are often blurry. It is unusual for any single company to own and control assets at all three stages. Instead, it is more common for specialized companies to focus on one step in the process. But this three-part organization does provide a basic framework for studying this enormously complicated industry.

The upstream sector is where the process begins. It involves determining where petroleum is and then getting it out of the ground and into containers. Finding petroleum reserves is known as exploration. It is a time-consuming and high-cost practice that has no guarantee of success. A failed

The petroleum industry involves large, complicated facilities and infrastructure.

Workers drill exploratory wells to verify the presence of petroleum underground.

exploration could leave the company with nothing to show for its investment.

Exploration starts with the discovery of a lead, a geologic feature that implies the potential existence of an underground oil field. An obvious example of a lead would be oil that has reached Earth's surface and formed a visible pool, known as a seep. Such a visible sign is rare, though, so geologists seek less-obvious leads. These include the presence of particular types of rocks that are commonly associated with hydrocarbon deposits.

Getting the oil out of the ground requires drilling a deep hole known as a borehole. This involves erecting a drilling rig, which includes not only the drill itself but several other critical components. One is called a mud pump. During drilling, the mud pump channels fluid into the borehole to keep the drilling equipment cool and bring drilled-off bits up to the surface. A hoisting

A Company's Best Asset

Once a suitable location for petroleum extraction has been identified, a series of tests and surveys is run to determine how much is potentially beneath the surface. One of the most common methods involves seismic reflection, which sends seismic waves into the ground and then generates an image after those waves bounce back. If the results from surveying and testing are favorable, an exploration well is drilled to determine what kind of rock covers the petroleum deposits and how far drilling must go. The oil company's scientists can study the exploration well to generate rough estimates of how much petroleum it can expect to recover and what grade of petroleum will be extracted. In the United States, if an untapped reservoir turns out to be rich in oil, the company that found it has to file for a government license to claim it. Once that process is completed, the site is added to the company's portfolio. These claims are generally viewed as a petroleum company's most important assets.

system feeds piping into the hole as it is drilled to keep the walls of the borehole from collapsing. And there is a tower known as a derrick, which helps guide the piping and other equipment into the borehole and then remove them when the job is completed. Once a borehole reaches a reservoir, extraction can begin. At the earliest stage of an oil well's life cycle, the petroleum is relatively easy to extract because of natural pressure in the reservoir cavity, which drives the petroleum to the surface. As time passes, however, the pressure lowers. The extraction team compensates for this by injecting water or gases into the reservoir.

Extreme Extraction

When the lightest grades of hydrocarbon are drawn out and only heavier grades remain, heavy oil needs to be heated to make it less viscous and easier to bring up. Often steam or carbon dioxide is used for this process. Mixtures of various microbes have also proven successful in loosening enough oil molecules to increase levels of recovery. There is also an approach that sets fire to the remaining oil to decrease viscosity. With this method, the drillers accept a certain loss of quantity in order to extract the rest. Some of these late-stage procedures can be expensive. They are only used when petroleum prices are high enough to justify them. Otherwise, wells that still have a low percentage of unrecovered reserves may sit dormant until prices rise again. The controversial process of hydraulic fracturing, or fracking, involves using pressurized liquids to create new fissures. This not only makes it easier to extract oil but also allows drillers to reach deposits that would have been otherwise inaccessible.

The Trans-Alaska Pipeline stretches 800 miles (1,300 km) between Alaska's northern and southern coasts.

MIDSTREAM ELEMENTS

Once petroleum has been drawn out of the ground and put in containers, it is ready to enter the second sector of the industry, the midstream. This involves transporting it to the many places it needs to go before it can enter the third and final sector, downstream.

A common method of petroleum transport is by pipelines. The United States alone has more than 150,000 miles (240,000 km) of pipelines dedicated to petroleum.[1] Most petroleum pipes run underground, but some sections are elevated because of frost or rocky soil. Pipelines also cross bodies of water and follow bridges over valleys. Pumping stations spaced at intervals maintain a steady flow. One of the downsides of pipeline transport is that segments tend to be vulnerable to intentional or accidental disruptions and leaks. These can result in extensive environmental damage.

Another method of transport is by oil tankers. These massive oceangoing vessels can be as long as 1,500 feet (460 m) and can carry as much as approximately two million barrels of crude oil.[2] Oil tankers are slow but economical. They can carry much greater quantities in a single trip than any other mode of transport.

Railways can also move petroleum in large volumes. Tank cars, specially designed to contain fluids, can be large enough to hold more than 500 barrels each.[3] This might not sound like much in comparison to a tanker, but it allows companies to cheaply transport oil long distances on land.

Trucks of varying sizes and classes can also be used to transport oil. However, they are usually reserved for refined petroleum products. Under certain circumstances, many are capable of moving crude oil for short distances. But their capacity limits make long-range transport impractical.

DOWNSTREAM ELEMENTS

The last stage of the petroleum industry involves processing the petroleum into its refined forms, which are then ready for sale to the customer. The core of this stage is the refining process. A

Tanker trucks distribute refined gasoline to gas stations.

typical oil refinery is usually a large facility occupying hundreds of acres. From the outside, it can look like an endless maze of pipes and towers. At least one of these towers will have a flame at the top. This is called a gas flare. It often indicates the burning of excess gases that cannot be collected.

Crude oil is refined through numerous processes. The primary process, fractional distillation, separates crude into multiple products. It takes place in a tall column. The refinery operators gradually increase the temperature of the crude, causing each component in the crude to reach its natural boiling point and exit the column. Lighter products, such as propane, have low boiling

Further Steps in Refinement

Some petroleum products go through further steps before they are ready for sale. Hydrodesulfurization, for example, removes sulfur, which is often found in oil in high quantities. The chemically induced sweetening process removes any remaining sulfurs. This allows the by-product to burn more cleanly. Another process is isomerization, which alters the order of atoms in a molecule. One use of isomerization is to increase the quality of gasoline and make it burn with greater efficiency.

points and will emerge early in the process. Kerosene, used as jet fuel, and gasoline, used as fuel in automobiles, come out soon after. Those that come out at the highest temperatures are the heaviest, such as lubricating oil and petroleum jelly. Another heavy product, bitumen, is used in the creation of asphalt.

The weight of each by-product results from the length of its carbon chain, the number of carbon atoms in each molecule. The longer the chain is, the heavier the by-product. Since the lighter by-products are often more valuable, many refineries also have equipment that can fracture the molecules of the heavier by-products into lighter ones through a process called cracking.

After a petroleum product has reached the end of the refining process, it is ready for distribution and sale. Many of the same methods used to transport the crude will be used in this final step of the downstream stage. Railcars and large-scale trucks play the biggest role in transporting products such as gasoline, though some by-products are sent overseas in tanker ships.

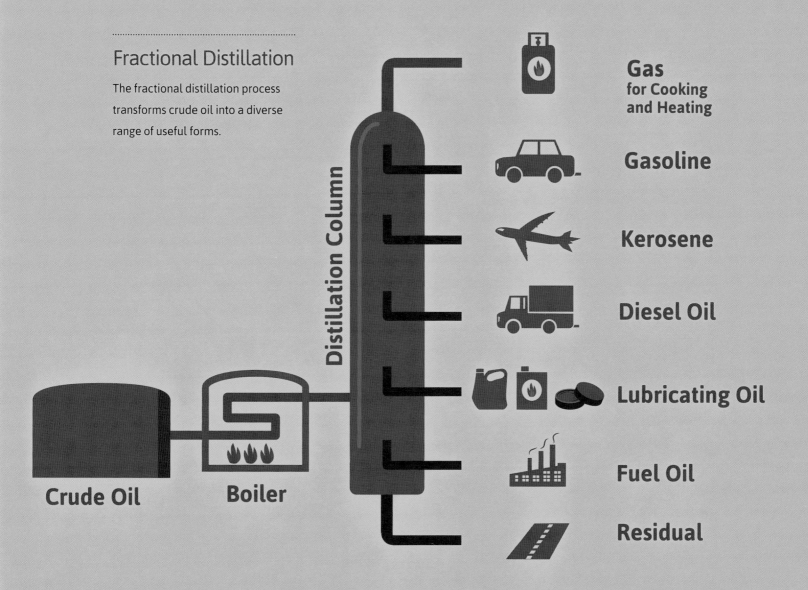

Fractional Distillation

The fractional distillation process transforms crude oil into a diverse range of useful forms.

Distillation Column

Gas
for Cooking and Heating

Gasoline

Kerosene

Diesel Oil

Lubricating Oil

Fuel Oil

Residual

Crude Oil

Boiler

8 | PETROPOLITICS

Few resources have played a more significant role in the delicate diplomacy of geopolitics during the last 100 years than petroleum. This black, oily substance has brought some economies crashing down while elevating others. It has been a driving factor in launching war and negotiating peace. It has turned enemies into allies. And it has built a bridge between the East and the West, though this connection is often unsteady. As more nations discover their own reserves and decide how best to use them, today's petropolitics continue to be as tense, unpredictable, and stormy as ever.

MORE OPTIONS, MORE POWER

A significant reduction in US oil imports, resulting from higher domestic production, has resulted in a much stronger US position on the global stage, as well as a significantly weaker position for some of the country's overseas suppliers. The United States has been the world's largest consumer of petroleum products for decades, making it an ideal customer for petroleum-producing nations. Some of these countries rely heavily on petroleum exports.

Crude oil has led to technological innovations, international conflicts, and environmental disasters.

Massive tanker ships owned by Saudi Aramco transport the company's oil from Saudi Arabia to countries around the world.

SAUDI ARAMCO

The largest energy company of any kind in the world is Saudi Aramco, headquartered in Dhahran, Saudi Arabia. It was established in 1933 following an oil agreement signed between Saudi Arabia and the Standard Oil Company of California. In 1948, the company discovered the Ghawar oil field, which has since proven to be one of the largest oil reserves in the world. It produces approximately 6 million barrels per day.[1] It is responsible for approximately 63 percent of Saudi Arabia's total petroleum output.[2] Saudi Aramco has more than 60,000 employees and annual revenues of more than $350 billion.[3]

One of the world's top petroleum-producing nations is Saudi Arabia. In 2015, petroleum sales accounted for 90 percent of the country's export income.[4] In May 2003, the US imported 71,461,000 barrels of crude from Saudi Arabia. By May 2015, that number dropped to 37,518,000.[5] With the US need for Saudi oil on a clear downward trajectory, Saudi Arabia's negotiating power diminished.

Another factor that changed US oil habits is the availability of oil from other markets. This has benefited the United States and these other nations. The United States becomes less dependent on a few major players. And in many instances, the oil revenues these smaller countries are now earning have enabled them to improve infrastructure, education, and health care. They have also reinvested some of their oil profits back into the industry, leading to new and improved technologies that will enable greater yields from their native reserves. The more prominent these minor players become, the fewer opportunities there are for major oil-producing nations to use their reserves as political leverage.

A Diminishing Dependency

There is a popular contemporary myth that the United States is hopelessly dependent upon Middle Eastern petroleum. In reality, the number one supplier of petroleum for the United States is itself. This has been the case for many years. By 2014, the United States had become the top oil producer in the world. In 2015, it produced an average of 13.7 million barrels a day, compared to Saudi Arabia's 11.9 million and Russia's 11 million.[6] When imported petroleum is needed in the United States, it is commonly supplied by Canada. In 2015, only approximately 24 percent of the petroleum used in the United States came from outside sources. This was the lowest level in nearly 50 years.[7]

BECOMING A PLAYER IN THE BIG GAME

The economic elevation of a country after it discovers oil under its territory often causes radical changes in that country's society. Not all of those changes are positive. Entering the petroleum industry can lead to numerous benefits, but it can also create new problems.

A dramatic example of this can be seen in Equatorial Guinea. Before 1996, the African nation had an economy hobbled by years of dictatorial rule. Its revenues were generated mostly by the agricultural sector. Then significant oil reserves were discovered, industrialized nations took interest, and the country's fortunes improved rapidly. Oil exploration had begun there in the late 1980s, but it was not until the 1990s that the economy began benefiting from it. From 1996 to 2000, the annual economic growth averaged 38.3 percent, a remarkable figure.[8] By comparison, the US economy did not grow faster than 6.5 percent in any year during this period.[9]

Equatorial Guinea's President

There is abundant evidence that a portion of Equatorial Guinea's newfound wealth ends up in the bank accounts of its president, Teodoro Obiang Nguema Mbasogo, and his family. A report by the Center for Public Integrity stated the president and his family were purchasing multimillion-dollar homes in the United States while many of their own citizens starved. Meanwhile, other nations appear to be turning a blind eye toward allegations of human-rights abuses in the country because they have profited from the country's reserves. Despite numerous attempts by the United States to persuade Obiang to improve his nation's human-rights record, little actual change has taken place.

Despite the nation's oil wealth, most people in Equatorial Guinea still live in poverty.

In 1996, Equatorial Guinea was producing approximately 6,000 barrels per day.[10] By 2014, with its industry boosted by both foreign and domestic investment, it averaged approximately 270,000 barrels per day, making it the sixth-largest producer in Africa and the thirty-fourth largest in the world.[11]

Royal Dutch Shell is best known to the public for its chain of thousands of Shell gas stations in the United States and other countries.

ROYAL DUTCH SHELL

Royal Dutch Shell has been a major player in the petroleum business since it was founded in 1907. Its true beginnings date to 1833, when London shopkeeper Marcus Samuel began selling imported shells because of their popularity at the time. This led to an import-export company that eventually adopted the name Shell. The corporation later ventured into the shipping business, particularly to meet the growing demand for petroleum later in the 1800s. Today, Royal Dutch Shell is headquartered in The Hague, Netherlands. Although its revenue dropped more than 50 percent from 2014 to 2015 due in large part to tumbling oil prices, it still earned a healthy $10.7 billion in that year.[1,2]

However, the discovery of oil has not benefited many of its citizens. According to the organization Human Rights Watch, little of the nation's petroleum wealth has been spent on critical programs such as health care and education. Instead, it has flowed to those who are already rich. Roughly half the country's population has no access to clean water. Approximately one-third of its children have growth problems stemming from malnutrition. Only approximately two in three children enroll in primary school.[13] Equatorial Guinea's vaccination rates are among the worst in the world. And there are broad areas of the country where electricity is either unreliable or unavailable. The story of Equatorial Guinea provides a striking illustration of how petroleum wealth, while enriching the oil industry, does not necessarily trickle down to a nation's average citizens.

9 | TODAY AND TOMORROW

Gasoline is the most widely used by-product of petroleum. In the United States alone, approximately 46 percent of crude oil is refined into gasoline for automobiles, trucks, construction machinery, farming equipment, landscaping equipment, and other land vehicles.[1] Approximately another 40 percent is used to power other vehicles, such as airplanes and cargo vessels.[2] The remaining percentage, while relatively small, is critical in the manufacturing of thousands of everyday items. They include tires, glue, paint, tape, yarn, dishes, cups, combs, dentures, candles, umbrellas, balloons, DVDs, and crayons, to name just a few.

The average person's life would be very different without these products. Toothbrushes and some toothpastes contain petroleum by-products. So do many shampoos, conditioners, soaps, and deodorants. Showering would be a challenge because most plumbing now uses durable plastic pipes made from petroleum. It would be difficult to get to school because the tires on buses, cars, and bicycles require petroleum. The bus also would not get far without gasoline in the tank or lubricating oil in the engine. A student requiring glasses might not be able to read in school, because lenses as well as many frames are made using petroleum.

Transportation continues to be the largest single use of petroleum products.

And without petroleum, schools would not have computers, monitors, or printers. Back home, the air conditioner cannot work in the summer and the furnace cannot work in the winter without petroleum. Food cannot be cooked, because petroleum by-products are used in barbecues, microwaves, and stoves. Sleeping would be a challenge since many sheets and blankets are made from fabrics that use petroleum. So are many kinds of clothing.

Electric cars, such as those made by Tesla, represent an attempt to shift the transportation sector away from petroleum.

PETROLEUM AND CLIMATE CHANGE

The consumption of petroleum products has resulted in the release of carbon dioxide into the atmosphere, contributing significantly to global climate change. Carbon dioxide exists in the atmosphere under natural conditions. However, burning fossil fuels releases a tremendous amount of it, increasing the

Peak Oil

There is a limited amount of oil underground. Eventually, the oil industry will reach a point at which the amount of petroleum it extracts reaches a high point. Petroleum extraction will then enter a continuous decline. This point is known as peak oil. It is unclear when peak oil will occur. According to a 2014 report by the company British Petroleum, there was enough oil left to satisfy needs at the current rate of consumption for more than 50 years.[5] However, there are many factors that could extend the life of the petroleum industry. Improved energy efficiency in petroleum-using products, newly discovered reserves, reduced demand due to alternative energy sources, and better extraction techniques could allow humanity to stretch its remaining oil supplies further.

percentage of the gas in the atmosphere. Earth is capable of absorbing excess carbon dioxide using trees and other plants. But it cannot keep up with such large amounts. The carbon dioxide builds up in the atmosphere, where it retains heat from the sun rather than allowing it to reflect back into space. This phenomenon is known as the greenhouse effect. It causes the gradual warming of the planet.

Climate change activists shut down an oil distribution train terminal in Oregon in 2014.

The generation of electricity is responsible for the largest share of carbon dioxide emissions, at approximately 37 percent.[3] Transportation is a close second, accounting for approximately 31 percent.[4] Petroleum products, including gasoline, are widely used in vehicles.

In both electricity generation and transportation, nations and corporations are working to replace oil and other fossil fuels. They are seeking energy sources that are more sustainable and better for the environment. Wind, solar, and hydroelectric power are three major

alternative sources for electricity generation. Electric cars, which can be charged from these clean sources of power, are alternatives to gasoline-powered vehicles. However, by 2016 most of the world's electricity and transportation were still powered by fossil fuels, including oil. Transitioning to different sources of power will take major investments of time, research, effort, and money.

THE FUTURE

The future of petroleum is impossible to predict. There does not appear to be any risk of global supplies running out in the near future, but it is clear there is a finite amount of oil in the ground. At the same time, the damage petroleum use is causing to the environment and climate cannot be disregarded.

Oil Spills

Oil spills occur when petroleum is transported from one place to another. Shipwrecks, train derailments, leaks, explosions, and other disasters can trigger oil spills. As oil seeps into the environment, it can harm plants or animals. The worst spill on record occurred in Kuwait during the Gulf War (1990–1991). In this instance, the spill was the product of intentional actions. Iraqi forces, eager to slow the progress of US troops, opened pipelines and well valves, allowing more than 240 million gallons (900 million L) to pour into the Persian Gulf.[6] This resulted in an oil slick roughly the size of the island of Hawaii.

Another major spill occurred in 2010, when an oil rig off the United States' Gulf Coast exploded. This resulted in the deaths of 11 workers and the underwater release of more than 210 million gallons (795 million L) of crude.[7] Oil flowed out of the uncovered borehole for approximately three months, damaging the environment, killing plants and animals, and paralyzing the local fishing and tourism industries.

Much of the innovation in the oil industry involves companies finding ways to extract petroleum from sources that were previously thought to be of little value. Heavy oil and oil shale are two good examples of this. Heavy oil is more difficult and expensive to refine than lighter

Fueling Options

The idea of reducing global reliance on petroleum has been around for decades, and from it has come a great deal of research on alternative fuels. One that is frequently mentioned is ethanol. It is a biofuel produced from feedstock, usually from items such as corn, sugar, and potatoes. There is no doubt ethanol has significant advantages. Since it comes from plants, it is a renewable resource. However, it is not as energy-dense as gasoline. In a typical car, 1 gallon (3.8 L) of gas provides about the same energy as 1.5 gallons (5.7 L) of ethanol.[8]

grades. Nevertheless, there are huge untapped deposits of it around the world, including in Venezuela and Canada. Oil shale is a type of sedimentary rock that can produce a dark hydrocarbon liquid when subjected to high temperatures. The resulting liquid can be used in place of conventional crude. However, it is so costly that most companies have not considered the process worthwhile. But as with heavy oil, there are giant reserves of oil shale around the world, including many in the United States.

The hills of western Colorado contain deposits of oil shale.

Companies are also searching for new sources of petroleum. These efforts have continued to stir up controversy among those who believe the conversion to alternative energy sources should start now. However, transitioning the world's economy and infrastructure away from oil will not be an easy process. For more than a century, the world has run on oil. And for the foreseeable future, it will remain a critical component of the planet's energy supply.

OIL PRODUCTION 2016[9]

6
CANADA
3.8 million barrels
per day

3
UNITED STATES
9.2 million barrels
per day

10
VENEZUELA
2.4 million barrels
per day

RUSSIA
10.5 million barrels
per day

IRAQ
4.3 million barrels
per day

CHINA
4.1 million barrels
per day

**SAUDI
ARABIA**
10 million barrels
per day

**UNITED
ARAB EMIRATES**
2.7 million barrels
per day

IRAN
3.5 million barrels
per day

KUWAIT
2.5 million barrels
per day

Timeline

1859

Edwin Drake strikes oil in Titusville, Pennsylvania, leading to the Pennsylvania oil rush and the start of the modern petroleum industry.

1870

John D. Rockefeller and his partners found the Standard Oil Company in Cleveland, Ohio. Standard will go on to monopolize the petroleum industry, but also organize and standardize it for the first time.

1885

German engineer Karl Benz builds the first automobile powered by a gas-powered internal combustion engine.

1908

Oil is discovered in Iran by the Anglo-Persian Oil Company, beginning a relationship between Iran and the United Kingdom that will be marked by tension in the years ahead.

1911

Rockefeller's Standard Oil Company is broken into 34 smaller companies.

1913

Friedrich Karl Rudolf Bergius invents a process for creating a light synthetic fuel from bituminous coal; William Burton and Robert Humphreys of Standard Oil develop thermal cracking, which breaks down heavy petroleum molecules.

1914

World War I begins; Winston Churchill, later the United Kingdom's prime minister, makes the decision to convert all British naval ships to oil.

1939

World War II breaks out in Europe. Oil, now deeply integrated into the world economy, plays a major role.

1960

After meeting in Baghdad, Iraq, the nations of Iran, Iraq, Kuwait, Saudi Arabia, and Venezuela agree to form an organization known as the Organization of Petroleum Exporting Countries (OPEC) to counter the dominance of Western oil companies.

1973

In response to US support of Israel during the Yom Kippur War, OPEC raises prices and cuts production, leading to severe gasoline shortages as well as other economic difficulties.

1975

In response to the 1973 oil crisis, the United States establishes the Strategic Petroleum Reserve—a sizable supply of petroleum earmarked for use during times of emergency.

1990

Saddam Hussein's invasion of Kuwait leads to a significant spike in oil prices and sets the stage for an eventual conflict between Iraq and the United States known as the Gulf War.

2008

During the global financial crisis, the price of oil reaches an all-time high of $135 per barrel.

2015

Following the lifting of sanctions against Iran in return for abandoning its nuclear weapons program, a glut of oil fills the market and drives prices steeply downward.

Essential Facts

IMPACT ON HISTORY

The effect that petroleum has had on humankind is immeasurable. It has enabled transportation, electricity, durable plastics, heating, lighting, and more. But the quest for petroleum has also led to global political tension, divided alliances, and even wars. Petroleum extraction has damaged ecosystems, and burning the resulting fuels has driven climate change. The world is making efforts to transition away from petroleum, but it will remain an essential source of energy for a long time to come.

KEY FIGURES

▶ Edwin Drake struck oil in Titusville, Pennsylvania, in 1859, launching the modern petroleum industry.

▶ Ida Tarbell was an early investigative journalist whose father went bankrupt because of John D. Rockefeller's predatory practices. She wrote a series of articles exposing Rockefeller, which contributed to his company's downfall.

▶ John D. Rockefeller founded Standard Oil, which was later broken up by the US government for monopolistic practices.

▶ Karl Benz was a German inventor, in 1885, of the first automobile powered by an internal combustion engine.

▶ President Richard M. Nixon signed the Emergency Petroleum Allocation Act following the Yom Kippur War in 1973.

KEY STATISTICS

▸ Refracking allowed 80 wells that were drilled in North Dakota in 2008 and 2009 to produce roughly 30 percent more oil than they had previously.

▸ Following the landmark court case *The Standard Oil Company of New Jersey, et al. v. The United States*, John D. Rockefeller's Standard Oil Company was broken into 34 smaller companies.

▸ In 2008, the price of crude oil reached its highest point ever—$135 per barrel.

▸ In the United States, approximately 46 percent of every barrel of crude oil is refined into gasoline for automobiles and other vehicles. Approximately another 40 percent is used to power larger craft such as airplanes and cargo vessels.

▸ A 2014 report by British Petroleum stated there was enough oil left to satisfy global needs at the current rate of consumption for more than 50 years.

QUOTE

"Oil, the blood of the Earth, was the blood of victory. . . . Germany had boasted too much of its superiority in iron and coal, but it had not taken sufficient account of our superiority in oil. . . . As oil had been the blood of war, so it would be the blood of the peace."

—*Henry Bérenger, French senator, speaking in 1918 following World War I*

Glossary

anticompetitive

Having the effect of reducing or discouraging competition.

barrel

A standard amount of petroleum equal to 42 gallons (158.9 L).

borehole

A hole dug into the earth, especially one made while exploring for oil.

commodity

Something that has value and is bought and sold.

consortium

A group of companies or nations that cooperate.

crude oil

Petroleum that has not yet been refined.

destroyer

A type of small, fast warship that protects larger vessels.

embargo

A government order that restricts the trade of commodities or goods.

extraction

The process of removing raw petroleum from underground.

geopolitics

The study of how geography and economics affect international policies and events.

glut

An excessive supply of something.

hydrocarbon

A substance containing only hydrogen and carbon.

hydroelectric

Having to do with the use of moving water to generate electricity.

monopoly

Exclusive control over a commodity or service.

reserve

An untapped amount of oil lying beneath Earth's surface.

sanction

An action taken to punish a country or force it to follow international laws.

seep

A spot on the ground where liquid oozes to the surface.

synthetic

Something made by humans.

viscosity

The thickness of a liquid.

Additional Resources

SELECTED BIBLIOGRAPHY

Hedges, Martin. *Rockefeller: Lord of Oil*. London, UK: Endeavour, 2013. Print.

Maugeri, Leonardo. *The Age of Oil: The Mythology, History, and Future of the World's Most Controversial Resource*. Westport, CT: Praeger, 2006. Print.

Yergin, Daniel. *The Prize: The Epic Quest for Oil, Money, and Power*. New York: Simon, 1991. Print.

FURTHER READINGS

Farrell, Courtney. *The Gulf of Mexico Oil Spill*. Minneapolis, MN: Abdo, 2011. Print.

Hamen, Susan E. *John D. Rockefeller: Entrepreneur & Philanthropist*. Minneapolis, MN: Abdo, 2011. Print.

Marrin, Albert. *Black Gold: The Story of Oil in Our Lives*. New York: Knopf, 2012. Print.

WEBSITES

To learn more about Big Business, visit **booklinks.abdopublishing.com**. These links are routinely monitored and updated to provide the most current information available.

FOR MORE INFORMATION

For more information on this subject, contact or visit the following organizations:

The Organization of the Petroleum Exporting Countries
Helferstorferstrasse 17, A-1010
Vienna, Austria
+43-1-21112-3302
http://www.opec.org/opec_web/en/

OPEC is a representative group of oil-producing nations that works to coordinate policies among its members to ensure fairness and stability in global petroleum markets.

The Society of Petroleum Engineers
222 Palisades Creek Drive
Richardson, TX 75080
972-952-9393
http://www.spe.org

The SPE works to share and advance knowledge concerning all upstream aspects of the petroleum industry, including exploration, drilling, and extraction.

US Energy Information Administration
1000 Independence Avenue Southwest
Washington, DC 20585
202-586-8800
http://www.eia.gov

The EIA's job is to collect, evaluate, and distribute data concerning the United States and all matters pertaining to energy, including consumption, importing, exporting, and production.

Source Notes

CHAPTER 1. THE PURSUIT OF INNOVATION

1. Alison Sider and Erin Ailworth. "Oil Companies Tap New Technologies to Lower Production Costs." *Wall Street Journal*. Wall Street Journal, 13 Sept. 2015. Web. 14 July 2016.

2. Brad Tuttle. "$1.50 Gas Prices Are Here—and $1 Per Gallon Could Be Next." *Money*. Time, 30 Nov. 2015. Web. 14 July 2016.

3. "2015 Gas Prices Second-Cheapest in a Decade: AAA Year-End Gas Price Report." *NewsRoom*. AAA, 2015. Web. 14 July 2016.

4. Robert Grattan. "Energy Companies Detail Hundreds More Layoffs." *FuelFix*. Houston Chronicle, 1 Feb. 2016. Web. 14 July 2016.

5. Alison Sider and Erin Ailworth. "Oil Companies Tap New Technologies to Lower Production Costs." *Wall Street Journal*. Wall Street Journal, 13 Sept. 2015. Web. 14 July 2016.

6. Dan Murtaugh, Lynn Doan, and Bradley Olson. "Refracking Is the New Fracking." *Bloomberg*. Bloomberg, 7 July 2015. Web. 14 July 2016.

7. "Oil and Gas Extraction." *Bureau of Labor Statistics*. US Department of Labor, 2016. Web. 14 July 2016.

CHAPTER 2. WHERE IT ALL BEGAN

1. "Feature Detail Report: Oil Creek." *Geographic Names Information System*. USGS, 2016. Web. 14 July 2016.

2. "Development of the Pennsylvania Oil Industry." *ACS*. ACS, 2016. Web. 14 July 2016.

3. Ibid.

4. Ibid.

5. "Early Crude Oil Production Levels and Pricing." *Oil 150*. Oil Region Alliance of Business, Industry & Tourism, n.d. Web. 14 July 2016.

6. Ibid.

CHAPTER 3. INCREASING DEMAND

1. Barbara Maranzani. "Bertha Benz Hits the Road." *History*. History Channel, 5 Aug. 2013. Web. 14 July 2016.

2. Charles W. Carey. *American Inventors, Entrepreneurs, and Business Visionaries*. New York: Facts on File, 2002. Print. 104.

3. "Ida Tarbell." *Biography*. Biography, 2016. Web. 14 July 2016.

4. Steve Weinberg. *Taking on the Trust: How Ida Tarbell Brought Down John D. Rockefeller and Standard Oil*. New York: Norton, 2008. Print. 225.

5. "Sherman Anti-Trust Act of 1890." *Society for Human Resource Management*. Society for Human Resource Management, 3 Dec. 2008. Web. 14 July 2016.

CHAPTER 4. OIL AND WARFARE

1. Erik J. Dahl. "Naval Innovation: From Coal to Oil." *JFQ*. JFQ, Winter 2000–2001. Web. 14 July 2016.

2. "The Blood of Victory: WWI." *Oil: International Evolution*. Pennsylvania State University, 2015. Web. 14 July 2016.

3. Ibid.

4. Saleem Hassan Ali. *Treasures of the Earth: Need, Greed, and a Sustainable Future*. New Haven, CT: Yale UP, 2009. Print. 119.

5. Franklin D. Roosevelt. "Appointment of Harold L. Ickes as Petroleum Coordinator for National Defense." *American Presidency Project*. American Presidency Project, 2016. Web. 14 July 2016.

6. "Styrene-Butadiene Rubber." *Encyclopaedia Britannica*. Encyclopaedia Britannica, 2016. Web. 14 July 2016.

Source Notes Continued

CHAPTER 5. THE RISE OF THE EAST

1. "General Information." *OPEC*. OPEC, May 2012. Web. 14 July 2016.

2. "Our Mission." *OPEC*. OPEC, 2016. Web. 14 July 2016.

3. "Six-Day War." *Encyclopaedia Britannica*. Encyclopaedia Britannica, 2016. Web. 14 July 2016.

CHAPTER 6. OIL SHORTAGES

1. "Oil Embargo, 1973–1974." *Office of the Historian*. US Department of State, n.d. Web. 14 July 2016.

2. Julian Lindley-French. *A Chronology of European Security and Defence, 1945–2007*. Oxford, UK: Oxford UP, 2008. Print. 114.

3. Charles Biderman. "Sky-High Oil Will Make US Go Broke." *Forbes*. Forbes, 23 June 2008. Web. 10 Aug. 2016.

4. "2008 Alaska Gasoline Pricing Investigation: Attorney General's Report." *Alaska Attorney General*. Alaska Attorney General, Jan. 2009. Web. 14 July 2016.

5. "OAPEC's Establishment." *OAPEC*. OAPEC, 2014. Web. 14 July 2016.

CHAPTER 7. HOW IT ALL WORKS TODAY

1. "Pipelines." *CIA World Factbook*. CIA, 2016. Web. 14 July 2016.

2. "Biggest Oil Tankers Overview." *Vessel Tracking*. Vessel Tracking, 2016. Web. 14 July 2016.

3. Nicole Friedman and Bob Tita. "The New Oil-Storage Space: Railcars." *Wall Street Journal*. Wall Street Journal, 28 Feb. 2016. Web. 14 July 2016.

CHAPTER 8. PETROPOLITICS

1. Gaurav Agnihotri. "A Closer Look at the World's 5 Biggest Oil Companies." *OilPrice*. OilPrice, 21 Apr. 2015. Web. 14 July 2016.

2. Rasoul Sorkhabi. "The King of Giant Fields." *GeoExPro*. GeoExPro, 2010. Web. 14 July 2016.

3. Gaurav Agnihotri. "A Closer Look at the World's 5 Biggest Oil Companies." *OilPrice*. OilPrice, 21 Apr. 2015. Web. 14 July 2016.

4. "Saudi Arabia." *CIA World Factbook*. CIA, 30 June 2016. Web. 14 July 2016.

5. "US Imports from Saudi Arabia of Crude Oil and Petroleum Products." *US Energy Information Administration*. USEIA, 30 June 2016. Web. 14 July 2016.

6. "World's Top Oil Producers." *Money*. CNN, 11 Feb. 2016. Web. 14 July 2016.

7. "How Much Oil Consumed by the United States Comes from Foreign Countries?" *US Energy Information Administration*. USEIA, 8 Mar. 2016. Web. 14 July 2016.

8. "Equatorial Guinea." *OECD*. OECD, 2002. Web. 14 July 2016.

9. "US GDP Growth Rate by Year." *Multipl*. Multipl, 2015. Web. 14 July 2016.

10. "Equatorial Guinea." *OECD*. OECD, 2002. Web. 14 July 2016.

11. "Equatorial Guinea." *US Energy Information Administration*. USEIA, Apr. 2015. Web. 14 July 2016.

12. "Fourth Quarter 2015 Results." *Shell Global*. Shell, 4 Feb. 2016. Web. 14 July 2016.

13. "World Report 2015: Equatorial Guinea." *Human Rights Watch*. Human Rights Watch, 2016. Web. 14 July 2016.

CHAPTER 9. TODAY AND TOMORROW

1. Stephanie Clifford. "Oil Oozes through Your Life." 25 June 2011. Web. 14 July 2016.

2. Ibid.

3. "Overview of Greenhouse Gas." *EPA*. EPA, 26 May 2016. Web. 14 July 2016.

4. Ibid.

5. Andy Tully. "BP's Latest Estimate Says World's Oil Will Last 53.3 Years." *OilPrice*. OilPrice, 11 July 2014. Web. 14 July 2016.

6. "10 Largest Oil Spills in History." *Telegraph*. Telegraph, 7 Oct. 2011. Web. 14 July 2016.

7. Ibid.

8. "Alcohol Fuel." *Petroleum.co.uk*. Petroleum.co.uk, 2015. Web. 14 July 2016.

9. "World's Top Oil Producers, First Three Months of 2016." *CNN Money*. CNN, 22 July 2016. Web. 23 Aug. 2016.

Index

ABOUT THE AUTHOR

Wil Mara is the award-winning author of more than 200 books, many of them educational titles for children. He began writing in the late 1980s with several nonfiction titles about herpetology, then branched into fiction in the mid-1990s. He has since authored more than a dozen novels.

DATE DUE

,ARDED